Know Your Neuro is dedicated to kids everywhere who are busy growing, strengthening and protecting their brain.

This book series could not have been realized without the unwavering excitement, inspiration and support of
Sally Waterfield, Taylor Collier,
Mooshi, Kali, Vishnu and Yuki.

www.KnowYourNeuro.org

Copyright © 2023 Dr Crystal Collier. All rights reserved.
Illustrations by Rachel Joanna
Manufactured in the United States of America

Library of Congress Cataloging-in-Publication Data
Collier, Crystal.
Know Your Neuro: Adventures of a Growing Brain
1. Substance use-Prevention 2. Youth-Drug Use 3. Education-Juvenile
Literature 4. High-risk behavior-Risky behavior

ISBN 978-1-7352957-7-0

KNOW YOUR NEURO:

Adventures of a Growing Brain

By:
Crystal Collier, PhD, LPC-S

Illustrated by:
Rachel Joanna

Your brain is a very important part of your body. You use your brain to see, hear, and feel things.

Everything you think, feel, and do happens in the brain!

The brain is so important that there are scientists who study all the different things it does!
I STUDY WHAT THE BRAIN DOES!
Neuroscience:
The study of the brain and how it functions.
They are called neuroscientists.

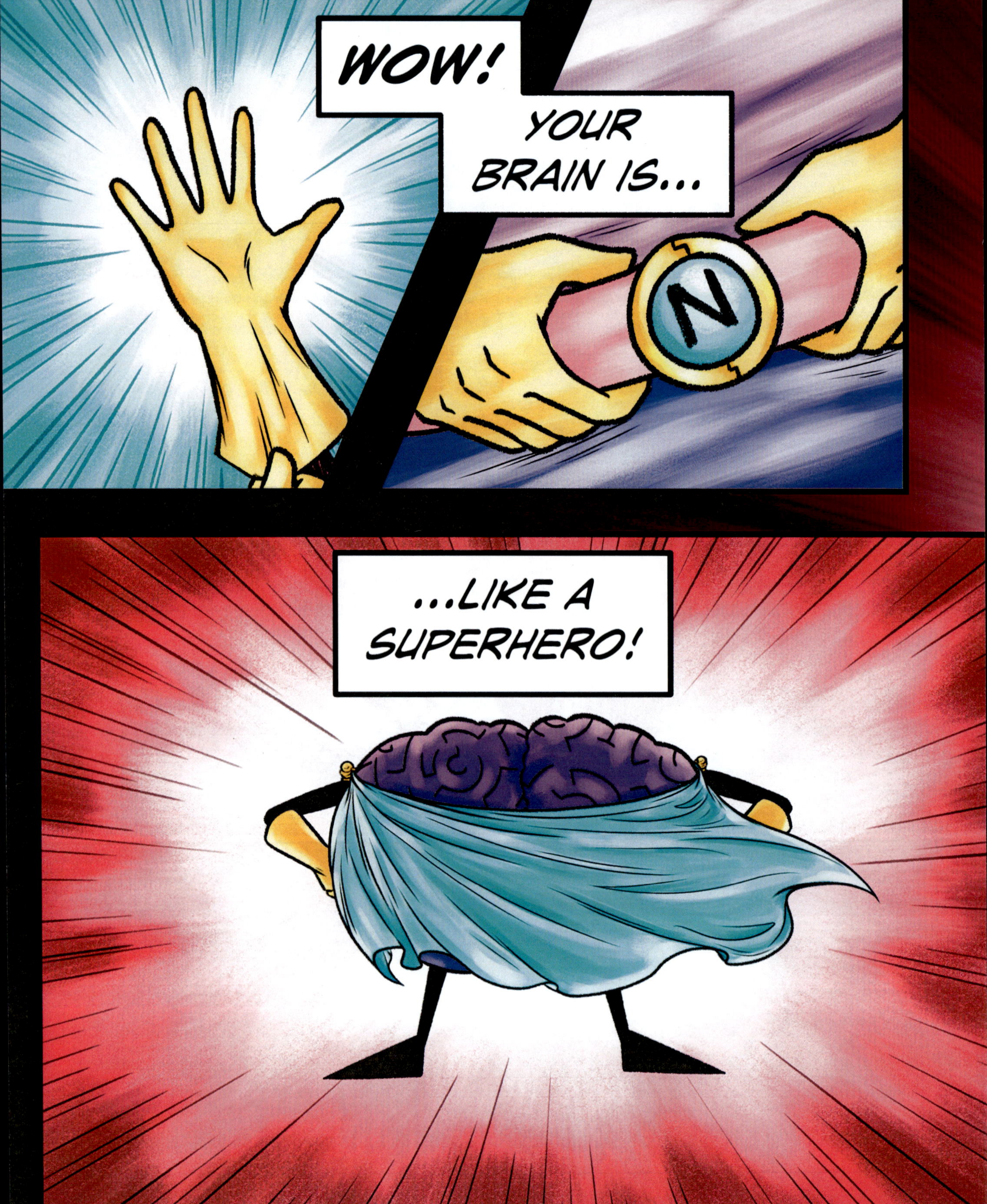

WOW!
YOUR BRAIN IS...
N
...LIKE A SUPERHERO!

...A SUPERHERO
NAMED...
NEURO!

Neuro is always learning
and growing to figure out ways
to keep you safe.

You can learn about Neuro
so that you can keep it safe!

Let's learn!

A really cool neuroscientist
who studies brains said,

WHAT PART OF THE CAR IS
THE ACCELERATOR AND WHAT PART
IS THE BRAKE?

Imagine if your brain looked like a car.

It would have a gas pedal called an accelerator to make you go and a brake pedal to make you stop.

Introducing....your accelerator! The gas pedal or accelertor is deep inside of your brain in an area called

The Limbic System is in charge of your 'accelerator'
the part that makes you GO,

and sometimes makes you go too fast!

Your Limbic System including
your accelerator are fully mature
and grown by the time you are 11 or 12!

The accelerator is famous for being really curious.

It helps you learn new things...

...like meeting new friends...

...playing a new sport, or how to do exciting new stuff.

But sometimes, it gets curious
about things you should
stay away from...

...like drugs, alcohol, unhealthy food,
using technology too much, being mean
to others, or looking at "Bad Pictures"
online.

That's where the thinking part
of your brain comes in.
It's called the Frontal Lobe,
and it is in charge of your brakes!

However, your Frontal Lobe is not
fully grown and developed until
around age 24 or 25!

Around 11 or 12, your brakes are just starting to get stronger and more reliable...

...depending upon how many times
you use them!
Your Frontal Lobe's brakes give you
enough time to think and make
a good decision before telling
the accelerator to go.

By practicing putting on the brakes...

...solve grown-up problems, show empathy toward others...

...and control impulses so you don't do risky things.

But the brain has a very important rule:
The "Use it or Lose it" Rule!

This means it needs
to practice making
good decisions
to grow positive thinking
and behavior skills--or it loses them!

Remember, you have a different brain than everyone else. That means you think differently than anyone else.

How will you strengthen your Frontal Lobe, so that your decisions will keep you and your Neuro safe from risky behavior, even if other people are making different decisions?

The more you use your Frontal Lobe's brakes by saying...

...helps your brain grow like it should!

MY STRONG BRAIN PLEDGE

for

____

I pledge to keep my brain strong and healthy. I will practice putting on my brakes to strengthen my Frontal Lobe. I will make good decisions, control my impulses, and say "no" to risky behavior to protect my brain as it grows and develops.

Every day I will:

☐ Use my Frontal Lobe brakes

☐ Slow down my Limbic System's accelerator

☐ Protect my brain from risky behavior

☐ Feed my brain healthy food

☐ Let my brain get plenty of sleep

☐ Keep it strong and growing

A Note from the Author

The Know Your Neuro series is designed to do two things:

1) Teach kids about their brain so that they will want to protect it and keep it strong.

2) Grow executive function skills.

Parents can do this too! Remember, risky behavior arrests healthy brain development and can slow down skill growth. For more resources, use the videos and handouts in

www.KnowYourNeuro.org

to be a Brain-Savvy Parent and Caregiver!

Crystal Collier, PhD, LPC-S

Follow MORE of Neuro's Adventures in:

Neuro Makes Good Choices
Neuro Sets Boundaries
Neuro Says No!
Neuro Feels Feelings
Neuro Accepts Their Body
Neuro Learns Self-Control
Neuro Grows Sharing Skills
Neuro Asks for Help
Neuro Grows Positive Self-Talk

Made in United States
North Haven, CT
28 February 2024